IRELAND

AN ILLUSTRATED YEARBOOK

1993

IRELAND

AN ILLUSTRATED YEARBOOK
1993

Illustrations · Kieran Doyle O'Brien

Text · Frank McDonald

Appletree Press

First published by The Appletree Press Ltd,
19-21 Alfred Street, Belfast BT2 8DL. Illustrations
© Kieran Doyle O'Brien, 1992. Text © Frank
McDonald, 1992. Printed in the EC. All rights
reserved. No part of this publication may be
reproduced or transmitted in any form or by any
means, electronic or mechanical, photocopying,
recording or in any information or retrieval system,
without prior permission in writing from the
publishers.

Front cover: Fanad Head, Co. Donegal
Back cover: Georgian Terrace, Cahir, Co. Tipperary

Endpapers (front): Rock of Cashel, Co. Tipperary
           (back): Roundstone, Co. Galway

ISBN 0 86281 346 8

Illustrations

Kieran Doyle O'Brien

Kieran Doyle O'Brien was born in Dublin and studied graphic design at the National College of Art and Design. Since 1981 he has worked as a painter and illustrator on public and private commissions in Ireland and abroad. In addition to numerous group shows, he has held one-man exhibitions at the Mount Street Gallery and the Malton Gallery in Dublin and at the Bell Gallery in Belfast. Previous collections of his illustrations have been published by Appletree Press as *Dublin: An Illustrated Yearbook* and *Ulster: An Illustrated Yearbook.*

Frank McDonald

Frank McDonald has been Environment Correspondent of *The Irish Times* since 1985. Dublin born, with an arts degree from University College, Dublin, he won the Award for Outstanding Work in Irish Journalism in 1980 for a series of articles entitled ''Dublin - What Went Wrong?'' He is also the author of two books, *The Destruction of Dublin* (1985) and *Saving the City* (1989). In 1988 he received a Lord Mayor's Millennium Medal for his work in making the public more aware of the architecture of the city.

Introduction

As a country, Ireland has not been particularly good at looking after its architectural heritage — perhaps because so much of it was regarded for so long as part of the legacy of the "800 years of oppression". This manifested itself most conspicuously in the burning of stately homes during earlier instalments of the Troubles — and also in the 1960s devil-may-care public attitude to the first assaults on the fabric of Georgian Dublin. It might even be said that we have a native instinct for vandalism!

Householders hardly think twice about throwing out their still-serviceable timber sash windows to make way for bright, new aluminium or uPVC versions. Windows have been rightly described as the "eyes" of a building. In most cases, they were designed with a particular size and glazing pattern in proportion to the house of which they form such an important element. Change the windows and you fundamentally alter the character of a building, even the architectural integrity of a whole period terrace.

Even now, despite growing public interest in our heritage, the Republic is alone among EC-member states in not giving grant aid towards the preservation of architecturally important listed buildings. And it was only within the past year that the penalties for demolishing such buildings were increased significantly in the wake of the appalling Drogheda Grammar School case. Northern Ireland fares rather better, with its Historic Buildings Council, grant schemes and the tremendous efforts of voluntary organisations such as Hearth.

In terms of recording Ireland's architectural heritage, the North also scores higher, with surveys by the Department of the Environment and the Ulster Architectural Heritage Society. In the South, by contrast, the Office of Public Works has just embarked on a series of surveys of historic towns to

fill in the many blank pages in our knowledge. Meanwhile, with some support from the State, the Irish Architectural Archive has continued its valuable work of documenting and photographing individual buildings for posterity.

Kieran Doyle O'Brien's carefully drawn watercolours may also be seen as a contribution to the public record, since their subjects — from Government Buildings in Merrion Street to thatched cottages in Connemara and gate lodges in the North — all form part of the tangible legacy left by previous generations of people on this island. If his evocation of the quality and often quirkily Irish character of these buildings helps to widen public appreciation of what we still hold, however tenuously, then so much the better.

Frank McDonald

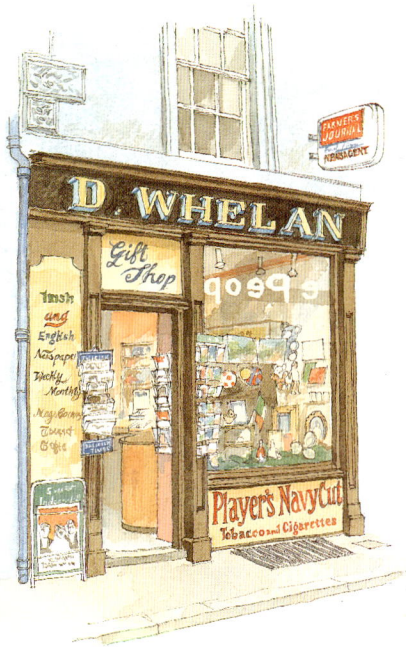

IRELAND

AN ILLUSTRATED YEARBOOK
1993

SEMBLY ROOMS

23 FRUITER

SOUTH BANK

1992-1993 DECEMBER-JANUARY

Monday Luan Montag Lundi ● Week 1

28

Tuesday Máirt Dienstag Mardi

29

Wednesday Céadaoin Mittwoch Mercredi

30

ASSEMBLY ROOMS
South Mall, Cork

The South Mall is Cork's most formal street, laid out in the late eighteenth century after the land was reclaimed from the Lee; for many years until it was arched over, a river channel ran through the middle of it. Though the street has suffered from insensitive redevelopment since the 1960s, it still has several relics of old decency, such as the Imperial Hotel. As a building, the Assembly Rooms are an eccentric piece of Victorian Romanesque, dating from 1860, as much at odds with the South Mall's later Georgian streetscape as any of the modern office blocks. First a hall and then a cinema, it is now in use as a restaurant.

Thursday Déardaoin Donnerstag Jeudi

31

Friday Aoine Freitag Vendredi
New Year's Day Lá Coille
Bank & public holiday

1

Saturday Satharn Samstag Samedi

2

Sunday Domhnach Sonntag Dimanche

3

Monday Luan Montag Lundi • Week 2

4

Tuesday Máirt Dienstag Mardi

5

Wednesday Céadaoin Mittwoch Mercredi

6

THATCHED HOUSE
Near Spiddal,
Co. Galway

The thatched cottage has long been one of the totems of Irish tourism, featuring prominently in Bord Failte brochures over the years. Tragically, few enough survive: thatchers can't be found so easily and, more significantly, the cottages themselves are inextricably associated with poverty and the Famine. The modern bungalow, one more ostentatious than the next, has long since replaced the cottage as the predominant house in rural Ireland — though it's still possible, even in the West where the losses have been higher than anywhere else, to find examples such as this cottage near Spiddal. But for how long?

Thursday Déardaoin Donnerstag Jeudi

7

Friday Aoine Freitag Vendredi

8

Saturday Satharn Samstag Samedi

9

Sunday Domhnach Sonntag Dimanche

10

1993   **JANUARY**

Monday Luan Montag Lundi • Week 3

11

Tuesday Máirt Dienstag Mardi

12

Wednesday Céadaoin Mittwoch Mercredi

13

FORMER RICHMOND HOSPITAL
Brunswick Street, Dublin

Perhaps the most impressive late Victorian building in Dublin, the former Richmond Hospital — which along with the adjoining Whitworth and Hardwicke was collectively known as St Laurence's — became redundant with the move out to Beaumont in 1987. And like several other inner-city hospitals, similarly afflicted by a relentless 1960s "rationalisation" plan, its doors were closed without any firm idea for an alternative use. After several years just lying there, it has now been rescued by TM enthusiasts Richard and Anne Quirke and brought back to life as a centre for Eastern-inspired complementary medicine, known as Ayuved.

Thursday Déardaoin Donnerstag Jeudi

14

Friday Aoine Freitag Vendredi

15

Saturday Satharn Samstag Samedi

16

Sunday Domhnach Sonntag Dimanche

17

Rich: Hoban
1780

1993

JANUARY

Monday Luan Montag Lundi ● Week 4

18

Tuesday Máirt Dienstag Mardi

19

Wednesday Céadaoin Mittwoch Mercredi

20

**GATE
Riverstown,
Co. Tipperary**

Riverstown is an attractive small village just across the Tipperary border from Birr, Co. Offaly. But even small villages in Ireland usually have a choice of watering holes, and Riverstown is no exception, with two pubs on its short main street. Located on the Little Brosna River which flows into the Shannon, it also has a narrow masonry arch bridge, which hopefully won't be ''improved'', and an eighteenth-century Big House — Riverstown — with a curiously charming Gothic gateway off the main street. Though the date stone beside it reads ''Rich. Hoban 1780'', the gateway is obviously much later — probably from the latter years of the nineteenth century.

Thursday Déardaoin Donnerstag Jeudi

21

Friday Aoine Freitag Vendredi

22

Saturday Satharn Samstag Samedi

23

Sunday Domhnach Sonntag Dimanche

24

Monday Luan Montag Lundi • Week 5

25

Tuesday Máirt Dienstag Mardi

26

Wednesday Céadaoin Mittwoch Mercredi

27

**PRESBYTERIAN
CHURCH
Loughbrickland,
Co. Down**

The counties of Ulster
have more churches and
chapels than anywhere
else in the country, mainly
because the
denominational affiliations
of the inhabitants are so
many and varied. Being
simple, honest folk, with
no tolerance of the pomp
and circumstance of Rome
or Canterbury, the
Presbyterians tended to
build simply too. This
meeting house in
Loughbrickland is even
simpler than most, with
virtually no adornment,
still less a soaring spire.
According to Marcus
Patton, it is ''utterly right
for its location, the hipped
roof and small-paned
windows plain but well
made, and the yew trees
in front sombre but neatly
clipped''.

Thursday Déardaoin Donnerstag Jeudi

28

Friday Aoine Freitag Vendredi

29

Saturday Satharn Samstag Samedi

30

Sunday Domhnach Sonntag Dimanche

31

Feabhra ● Februar ● Février

1993 FEBRUARY

Monday Luan Montag Lundi ● Week 6

1

Tuesday Máirt Dienstag Mardi

2

Wednesday Céadaoin Mittwoch Mercredi

3

STABLE BLOCK, BANTRY HOUSE
Co. Cork

Bantry House enjoys the most spectacular location of Ireland's stately homes. Dating from 1771, it is located on an elevated site with panoramic views southwards over Bantry Bay to the Caha Mountains, on the Beara Peninsula. Once the seat of the Earls of Bantry, it is still in the hands of the same family, through Clodagh and Egerton Shellswell-White. They were the first stately home-owners to open their house to the public, and it has proved to be an enduring tourist attraction as well as offering superb bed-and-breakfast accommodation. A Spanish Armada museum is being developed in the grounds.

Thursday Déardaoin Donnerstag Jeudi

4

Friday Aoine Freitag Vendredi

5

Saturday Satharn Samstag Samedi

6

Sunday Domhnach Sonntag Dimanche

7

1993   FEBRUARY

Monday Luan Montag Lundi ● Week 7

8

Tuesday Máirt Dienstag Mardi

9

Wednesday Céadaoin Mittwoch Mercredi

10

Thursday Déardaoin Donnerstag Jeudi

11

Friday Aoine Freitag Vendredi

12

Saturday Satharn Samstag Samedi

13

Sunday Domhnach Sonntag Dimanche

14

THE MALL
Westport, Co. Mayo

Unlike most Irish towns which tended to grow organically, Westport was at least partly planned in the late eighteenth century by the English architect James Wyatt, who also designed Castle Coole, outside Enniskillen, as well as remodelling Westport House. His patron was the 3rd Earl of Altamont, later 1st Marquess of Sligo (only because Mayo was already spoken for), a landlord with a serious interest in estate management. The pleasant tree-lined Mall on both sides of the Carrowbeg River, which flows through the town, and the unusual octagonal-shaped square, with its market house and town hall, are Wyatt's principal legacies.

1993

FEBRUARY

Monday Luan Montag Lundi ● Week 8

15

Tuesday Máirt Dienstag Mardi

16

Wednesday Céadaoin Mittwoch Mercredi

17

DRIMNAGH CASTLE
Co. Dublin

Dating from the thirteenth century, Drimnagh has the unique distinction of being the only medieval castle in Ireland with its moat still full of water. Sandwiched between the Naas Road and the Long Mile Road in Dublin's industrial belt, it might have been left to become another ivy-clad ruin. But after years of dereliction it was rediscovered by artist and conservationist Peter Pearson, who set about restoring it with the active involvement of FAS as well as the local community. And on a joyous sunny day in May 1991, President Robinson came to Drimnagh to mark the completion of the first phase of this heroic project.

Thursday Déardaoin Donnerstag Jeudi

18

Friday Aoine Freitag Vendredi

19

Saturday Satharn Samstag Samedi

20

Sunday Domhnach Sonntag Dimanche

21

Monday Luan Montag Lundi ● Week 9

22

Tuesday Máirt Dienstag Mardi

23

Wednesday Céadaoin Mittwoch Mercredi

24

FORMER MARKET HOUSE
Collon, Co. Louth

Collon was Speaker Foster's estate village and thus bears the mark of its landlord's hand — most astonishingly the Protestant church, dating from 1813, which was designed as an ambitious but economical copy of King's College Chapel in Cambridge. Collon's most picturesque feature is the charming group of buildings around the village green, whose centre-piece is this unusual market house, with its decorative barge-boards, cupola and clock. Though there is no record of when it was built, a plaque on the facade records that the clock was donated by the local vicar in 1822, probably not very long after the building was completed.

Thursday Déardaoin Donnerstag Jeudi

25

Friday Aoine Freitag Vendredi

26

Saturday Satharn Samstag Samedi

27

Sunday Domhnach Sonntag Dimanche

28

1993   MARCH

Monday Luan Montag Lundi ● Week 10

1

Tuesday Máirt Dienstag Mardi

2

Wednesday Céadaoin Mittwoch Mercredi

3

GATE LODGE
Ely, Co. Fermanagh

The Elys certainly got around — starting out in Rathfarnham Castle in Dublin, moving on to Ely House at the top of Hume Street, thence to Ely Castle on the lushly wooded shores of Lough Erne and, finally, to Loftus Hall, near the Hook Head in Co. Wexford. The latter move followed a spectacularly unfortunate incident in 1870 when Ely Castle, built less than fifty years earlier, was blown up as the climax of a wild party to mark the coming of age of the 4th Marquess of Ely. The Regency castle had been designed by William Farrell, who was also responsible for this fine neo-classical gate lodge, which has fortunately survived.

Thursday Déardaoin Donnerstag Jeudi

4

Friday Aoine Freitag Vendredi

5

Saturday Satharn Samstag Samedi

6

Sunday Domhnach Sonntag Dimanche

7

1993 **MARCH**

Monday Luan Montag Lundi ● Week 11

8

Tuesday Máirt Dienstag Mardi

9

Wednesday Céadaoin Mittwoch Mercredi

10

ULSTER BANK
College Green, Dublin

Irish cities and towns are
enormously enhanced by
their Victorian bank
buildings, all designed to
convey an image of solid
security to their genteel
customers. The Ulster
Bank in College Green is
one of the most ornate, an
exuberant piece of
nineteenth-century neo-
classicism, with a Parisian-
style roof to cap it all.
Sadly, the wonderful
barrel-vaulted porch
behind the high entrance
gates is all that survives
of its spectacular interior.
In the mid 1970s, for
some extraordinary
reason, the whole lot was
ripped out and replaced
with the sort of
anonymous modern
banking hall which can be
seen almost anywhere. No
doubt the bankers now
regret their error.

Thursday Déardaoin Donnerstag Jeudi

11

Friday Aoine Freitag Vendredi

12

Saturday Satharn Samstag Samedi

13

Sunday Domhnach Sonntag Dimanche

14

1993   MARCH

Monday Luan Montag Lundi ● Week 12

15

Tuesday Máirt Dienstag Mardi

16

Wednesday Céadaoin Mittwoch Mercredi
St Patrick's Day Lá Fhéile Phádraig
Bank & public holiday

17

**NORTHERN
CONSTITUTION
Coleraine, Co. Derry**

According to Alistair
Rowan in his book on the
architectural heritage of
North-West Ulster, the
quality which Coleraine
had at the turn of the
century has been
''systematically eroded by
needless road-widening,
the uncontrolled creation
of carparks, the shoddy
modernisation of shops
and offices, and a seeming
lack of concern for the
fate of its older buildings''
— a damning verdict
which could equally be
applied to some other Irish
cities and towns. Some
things of value survive,
however, such as the
Northern Constitution's
offices on Railway Road, a
pleasant arts-and-crafts
building circa 1900 in red
brick and terracotta.

Thursday Déardaoin Donnerstag Jeudi

18

Friday Aoine Freitag Vendredi

19

Saturday Satharn Samstag Samedi

20

Sunday Domhnach Sonntag Dimanche

21

1993

MARCH

Monday Luan Montag Lundi ● Week 13

22

Tuesday Máirt Dienstag Mardi

23

Wednesday Céadaoin Mittwoch Mercredi

24

TOWNSEND STREET
Skibbereen, Co. Cork

One of the joys of West
Cork, apart from the
scenery, is its towns and
villages, which always
seem to be more charming
than nearly everywhere
else. Some of the credit
for the appearance of
Kinsale, Clonakilty and
Skibbereen, with their
brightly painted buildings
and traditional-type
shopfronts, must go to
their chief architect/
planner Billy Houlihan. In
his inimitable way, he
brought town planning
down to ground level from
the dizzy heights of Cork
County Hall, persuading
people not only to look
after their properties a
little better but also to see
the towns as places to
live in, rather than merely
serving the interests of
commerce.

Thursday Déardaoin Donnerstag Jeudi

25

Friday Aoine Freitag Vendredi

26

Saturday Satharn Samstag Samedi

27

Sunday Domhnach Sonntag Dimanche

28

Márta-Aibreán ● März-April ● Mars-Avril

1993 MARCH-APRIL

Monday Luan Montag Lundi ● Week 14

29

Tuesday Máirt Dienstag Mardi

30

Wednesday Céadaoin Mittwoch Mercredi

31

COUNTY MUSEUM
The Mall, Armagh

According to Gavin
Stamp, the forthright
architectural historian,
Armagh ''remains one of
the finest Georgian cities
in Ireland'' and, possibly,
anywhere in these islands.
In spite of the
depredations of terrorists
and road engineers, it
retains an eighteenth-
century grandeur, though
the scale is relatively
modest compared to
Dublin. Its set piece is the
Mall, a lovely urban park
fringed by limestone-
fronted Georgian houses
as well as Gothic churches
or gospel halls, with the
courthouse and the gaol at
either end. Roughly in the
middle of the Mall is the
county museum, opened
in 1931, which was built
a century earlier as a
school.

Thursday Déardaoin Donnerstag Jeudi

1

Friday Aoine Freitag Vendredi

2

Saturday Satharn Samstag Samedi

3

Sunday Domhnach Sonntag Dimanche

4

1993   APRIL

Monday Luan Montag Lundi ● Week 15

5

Tuesday Máirt Dienstag Mardi

6

Wednesday Céadaoin Mittwoch Mercredi

7

JUVENILE COURT
Smithfield, Dublin

The issue of whether there should be courts for trying children is not one for discussion here; though, if there must be such facilities, it is fitting that they should be housed in a fine modern building such as this. Designed by award-winning architect John Tuomey while he was still employed by the Office of Public Works, it is respectful towards its neighbours — a red-brick Victorian house on one side and a stone warehouse on the other — without in any way imitating them. It also shows how Smithfield, potentially one of the finest spaces in Dublin, could be rescued from its current sorry state and pointed in a new direction.

Thursday Déardaoin Donnerstag Jeudi

8

Friday Aoine Freitag Vendredi
Good Friday
Bank holiday

9

Saturday Satharn Samstag Samedi

10

Sunday Domhnach Sonntag Dimanche
Easter Sunday Domhnach Cásca

11

1993　　　　　　　　　　　**APRIL**

Monday Luan Montag Lundi ● Week 16
Easter Monday Luan Cásca
Bank & public holiday

12

Tuesday Máirt Dienstag Mardi

13

Wednesday Céadaoin Mittwoch Mercredi

14

Thursday Déardaoin Donnerstag Jeudi

15

Friday Aoine Freitag Vendredi

16

Saturday Satharn Samstag Samedi

17

Sunday Domhnach Sonntag Dimanche

18

**GATE LODGE,
CASTLEDAWSON
Co. Derry**

Dawson Street in Dublin is named after Sir Joshua Dawson, the part-time property developer who built the Mansion House and who once served as Chief Secretary for Ireland. His family also gave its name to Castledawson, the estate village of their country seat at Moyola Park, a Georgian mansion built by Arthur Dawson in 1768 at the height of their fortunes. This Hansel-and-Grettel gate lodge, described by Marcus Patton as ''almost alarmingly pink against the surrounding trees'', is a Victorian Gothic creation, like so many gate lodges on Irish country estates — not just ornaments, but discreet defences, too.

1993   APRIL

Monday Luan Montag Lundi ● Week 17

19

Tuesday Máirt Dienstag Mardi

20

Wednesday Céadaoin Mittwoch Mercredi

21

KING-HARMON HOUSE
Boyle, Co. Roscommon

Thursday Déardaoin Donnerstag Jeudi

22

Ten years ago, Boyle's most impressive building was in such a dreadful state that there were trees growing out of its gutters and its vaulted interior was being used to store turf. For decades, of course, it had been a British barracks, which probably did not endear it to local people, and previously the town house of Boyle's most powerful landlords, the King-Harmons, the core of whose Rockingham estate is now better known as Lough Key Forest Park. In 1991 a major restoration of the palatial circa-1730 house was put in hand by architects Maura and Patrick Shaffrey, with aid from the EC, the National Heritage Council and the Getty Foundation.

Friday Aoine Freitag Vendredi

23

Saturday Satharn Samstag Samedi

24

Sunday Domhnach Sonntag Dimanche

25

Monday Luan Montag Lundi ● Week 18

26

Tuesday Máirt Dienstag Mardi

27

Wednesday Céadaoin Mittwoch Mercredi

28

Thursday Déardaoin Donnerstag Jeudi

29

MOONEY'S SHOP
High Street, Kilkenny

Kilkenny prides itself on looking after its heritage and, indeed, it is one of the few towns in Ireland with surviving examples of medieval houses. With a great castle, cathedral and abbey, as well as a street network which also dates from the Middle Ages, it is now well established as the country's premier medieval city. Behind the facade, however, things are changing, with plans for a major shopping centre to the rear of High Street and Parliament Street which will irrevocably alter the shape of the city. But at least Kilkenny still has many fine traditional shopfronts, such as Mooney's, among the proliferating parodies.

Friday Aoine Freitag Vendredi

30

Saturday Satharn Samstag Samedi

1

Sunday Domhnach Sonntag Dimanche

2

Monday Luan Montag Lundi ● Week 19

3

Tuesday Máirt Dienstag Mardi

4

Wednesday Céadaoin Mittwoch Mercredi

5

Thursday Déardaoin Donnerstag Jeudi

6

Friday Aoine Freitag Vendredi

7

Saturday Satharn Samstag Samedi

8

Sunday Domhnach Sonntag Dimanche

9

CHARLEMONT FORT
Co. Armagh

Not much is left of the once-impressive star-shaped fort built in 1602 by Lord Mountjoy at Charlemont, across the Blackwater from Moy, Co. Tyrone. After falling into Irish hands during the 1641 Uprising, it was regarrisoned by the English, who added massive earthworks to make the fort more secure in the event of another assault, and it remained in use as a military installation until 1858. Today, as Marcus Patton has noted, ''the entrance gates beyond an avenue of lime trees guard only a field of thistles and butterflies, while the walls to the north have nearly been breached by a bungalow''. Lord Mountjoy would not be amused.

Monday Luan Montag Lundi ● Week 20

10

Tuesday Máirt Dienstag Mardi

11

Wednesday Céadaoin Mittwoch Mercredi

12

Thursday Déardaoin Donnerstag Jeudi

13

Friday Aoine Freitag Vendredi

14

Saturday Satharn Samstag Samedi

15

Sunday Domhnach Sonntag Dimanche

16

PUBLIC LAVATORY
Youghal, Co. Cork

The often deplorable condition of public toilets throughout the country has been a perennial gripe among those concerned about Ireland's tourism prospects, provoking offended visitors to wonder about this darker side to our hospitality — not to mention the precise meaning of *Fir* and *Mna*. The facilities in Youghal are of a standard mid twentieth-century type, with pebble-dashed concrete walls and basic accommodation inside. What made this lavatory unusual was the shark on its roof (now gone), evoking the town's seafaring traditions. Behind it, in dressed rubble stone, is the old gable-fronted market house.

Monday Luan Montag Lundi ● Week 21

17

Tuesday Máirt Dienstag Mardi

18

Wednesday Céadaoin Mittwoch Mercredi

19

GEORGIAN TERRACE
Cahir, Co. Tipperary

Contrary to popular impression, Georgian town architecture is not confined to Dublin or Limerick. Many Irish towns have fine terraces or squares, however small or truncated, indicating that some of their inhabitants did quite well for themselves during the Age of Enlightenment and the early decades of the nineteenth century. As a Butler town with the right allegiances, Cahir was well placed in any contest for prestige, producing such fine houses as this terrace on the banks of the River Suir. The recently restored Swiss Cottage, designed by John Nash in the Regency *cottage ornée* style, is just outside the town.

Thursday Déardaoin Donnerstag Jeudi

20

Friday Aoine Freitag Vendredi

21

Saturday Satharn Samstag Samedi

22

Sunday Domhnach Sonntag Dimanche

23

Monday Luan Montag Lundi ● Week 22

24

Tuesday Máirt Dienstag Mardi

25

Wednesday Céadaoin Mittwoch Mercredi

26

TEDCASTLE'S HUT
The Quay, Waterford

The best vantage point from which to view the quays in Waterford is the Ardree Hotel, high above the north bank of the River Suir; it also means that one cannot see the Ardree itself, which otherwise dominates the scene. Round and stocky Reginald's Tower is by far the oldest structure on the quays, which are largely lined with nineteenth-century commercial buildings and a few modern eyesores. To the rear are the contrasting profiles of Waterford's two cathedrals and the town's warren of medieval streets. Since most port activity has moved downstream, there is not much happening on the quays, which are now in danger of being turned into a carpark.

Thursday Déardaoin Donnerstag Jeudi

27

Friday Aoine Freitag Vendredi

28

Saturday Satharn Samstag Samedi

29

Sunday Domhnach Sonntag Dimanche

30

1993   MAY-JUNE

Monday Luan Montag Lundi ● Week 23

31

Tuesday Máirt Dienstag Mardi

1

Wednesday Céadaoin Mittwoch Mercredi

2

**WEST PIER
Dun Laoghaire,
Co. Dublin**

Of all the ports of arrival
in Ireland, with the
possible exception of
Cobh, Dun Laoghaire
continues to provide the
most captivating
panorama more than 150
years after the harbour
was completed — and
conversely, the sight of
the ''mailboat'' coming in
is still the most
memorable image of what
used to be the Borough of
Kingstown. Apart from the
largely Victorian skyline —
somewhat spoiled by
modern intrusions, such as
the shopping centre and
BIM's office block — it is
the harbour itself, with its
massive granite piers,
which make the deepest
impression . . . a sturdy
monument to engineer
John Rennie and the men
who built it.

Thursday Déardaoin Donnerstag Jeudi

3

Friday Aoine Freitag Vendredi

4

Saturday Satharn Samstag Samedi

5

Sunday Domhnach Sonntag Dimanche

6

Monday Luan Montag Lundi ● Week 24
Bank & public holiday

7

Tuesday Máirt Dienstag Mardi

8

Wednesday Céadaoin Mittwoch Mercredi

9

BRIDGE AT BANDON
Co. Cork

Bridges tend to be taken for granted, in Ireland more than most countries. We are only just recovering from the tendency to regard rivers as drains, which explains why so few buildings in Irish towns actually face the water. "Often it takes somebody, possessing a different attitude, to draw our attention to something right under our noses", Robert Ballagh wrote in his introduction to Michael Barry's book on Irish bridges, *Across Deep Waters*. But in Bandon they show rather more respect for the river, and this Methodist chapel, with its tall round-headed windows, seems almost tailor-made for its setting beside the bridge.

Thursday Déardaoin Donnerstag Jeudi

10

Friday Aoine Freitag Vendredi

11

Saturday Satharn Samstag Samedi

12

Sunday Domhnach Sonntag Dimanche

13

Monday Luan Montag Lundi ● Week 25

14

Tuesday Máirt Dienstag Mardi

15

Wednesday Céadaoin Mittwoch Mercredi

16

**FANAD HEAD
Co. Donegal**

It was Lord Grey who remarked glumly in 1914 that the lamps were going out all over Europe. Around the coast of Ireland, the lights may not be going out, but they are being automated, and the human contact between the old lighthouse keepers and the ships that pass in the night is no more. For several years the Commissioners of Irish Lights — whose responsibilities, unusually, straddle the Border — have been pursuing a determined policy of automation; at the time of writing there were only nine lighthouses left with their faithful keepers still on duty. Fanad Head, at the entrance to Lough Swilly, is among the many which are now on ''auto-pilot''.

Thursday Déardaoin Donnerstag Jeudi

17

Friday Aoine Freitag Vendredi

18

Saturday Satharn Samstag Samedi

19

Sunday Domhnach Sonntag Dimanche

20

1993   **JUNE**

Monday Luan Montag Lundi ● Week 26

21

Tuesday Máirt Dienstag Mardi

22

Wednesday Céadaoin Mittwoch Mercredi

23

GATE LODGE
Hillsborough, Co. Down

Hillsborough seems almost too pretty and well ordered to be in Ireland at all; it looks as if it might have been transplanted from Devon or somewhere in the English shires. Indeed, planning control is so rigorous that nearly every retail outlet resembles Ye Olde Curiosity Shoppe. But Hillsborough will always be associated with the signing in 1985 of the Anglo-Irish Agreement between Margaret Thatcher and Garret FitzGerald, with seething Unionists protesting at the gates of the castle. The picturesque character of the town is exemplified in this delightful gate lodge, one of a pair at the entrance of the eighteenth-century parish church.

Thursday Déardaoin Donnerstag Jeudi

24

Friday Aoine Freitag Vendredi

25

Saturday Satharn Samstag Samedi

26

Sunday Domhnach Sonntag Dimanche

27

1993

JUNE-JULY

Monday Luan Montag Lundi ● Week 27

28

Tuesday Máirt Dienstag Mardi

29

Wednesday Céadaoin Mittwoch Mercredi

30

Thursday Déardaoin Donnerstag Jeudi

1

PUB
Clara, Co. Offaly

Like a few other towns in the Midlands, Clara originated as a Quaker settlement, and though there are few Friends left, the town still has a well-planned look about it. Nearby is Clara Bog, one of the last surviving raised bogs in the entire area, where the flora and fauna are to be conserved rather than swept away by Bord na Mona's harvesters. Just outside the town, within sight of the railway line, is Clara's unusual Lourdes grotto which consists of an outsized chalice and host, rather than the more familiar representations of the Virgin Mary and Saint Bernadette seen in many parts of the country.

Friday Aoine Freitag Vendredi

2

Saturday Satharn Samstag Samedi

3

Sunday Domhnach Sonntag Dimanche

4

Monday Luan Montag Lundi ● Week 28

5

Tuesday Máirt Dienstag Mardi

6

Wednesday Céadaoin Mittwoch Mercredi

7

PHOENIX PARK LODGE
Dublin

The Phoenix Park is one of the three priceless legacies to Dublin of the Great Duke of Ormonde, Viceroy of Charles II, the others being the Liffey Quays and the Royal Hospital, Kilmainham. Since 1986, its 1,750 acres have been officially designated as a National Historic Park and, since then, the Office of Public Works has been directing its efforts to restore the park's historic landscape, in which Decimus Burton played a major creative role. Dotted through the park are some very important buildings, notably Aras an Uachtarain, and several lesser ones, such as this quaint keeper's lodge at the edge of the Fifteen Acres.

Thursday Déardaoin Donnerstag Jeudi

8

Friday Aoine Freitag Vendredi

9

Saturday Satharn Samstag Samedi

10

Sunday Domhnach Sonntag Dimanche

11

Monday Luan Montag Lundi ● Week 29

12

Tuesday Máirt Dienstag Mardi

13

Wednesday Céadaoin Mittwoch Mercredi

14

SLIGO ABBEY
Sligo

Ruins are an endemic and poignant feature of the Irish landscape. Even when Daniel Grose was drawing his pictures to catalogue the island's antiquities in the first decade of the nineteenth century, many of these relics were already in ruins — proof, according to Grose, that man's more durable works are only ''a little less evanescent than himself''. The more substantial, undoubtedly, are the remains of the monasteries, suppressed in the cause of the Reformation. Sligo Abbey, one of the more impressive of these monastic relics, was a Dominican friary dating from 1252 which was burned in 1641 by Sir Frederick Hamilton.

Thursday Déardaoin Donnerstag Jeudi

15

Friday Aoine Freitag Vendredi

16

Saturday Satharn Samstag Samedi

17

Sunday Domhnach Sonntag Dimanche

18

Monday Luan Montag Lundi ● Week 30

19

Tuesday Máirt Dienstag Mardi

20

Wednesday Céadaoin Mittwoch Mercredi

21

ICE CREAM SHOP
Bray, Co. Wicklow

Thursday Déardaoin Donnerstag Jeudi

22

Like many Victorian seaside towns in these islands, Bray has seen better times. Its heyday was around the turn of the century, stretching into the 1920s and 1930s when it was still popular to rent rooms in the lodging houses along the promenade for a summer holiday. Gradually, the dodgems and amusement arcades took over and Bray became a more tawdry place. But much of the town's Victorian and Edwardian architectural heritage still survives, and recently its quaint town hall was restored — after years of neglect — to house a variety of commercial uses. However, the line of the promenade has been disrupted by the development of an aquarium.

Friday Aoine Freitag Vendredi

23

Saturday Satharn Samstag Samedi

24

Sunday Domhnach Sonntag Dimanche

25

1993   JULY-AUGUST

Monday Luan Montag Lundi ● Week 31

26

Tuesday Máirt Dienstag Mardi

27

Wednesday Céadaoin Mittwoch Mercredi

28

ROYAL CORK YACHT CLUB
Cobh, Co. Cork

Like so many other historic buildings in Ireland, the former Royal Cork Yacht Club in Cobh was unaccountably left to go derelict and might even have been lost but for the determination of a handful of conservationists. They established the Sirius Project, with the aim of bringing the wonderful Italianate building back to life — though as an artist's centre rather than as a yacht club. This most laudable scheme neatly dovetails with the co-ordinated effort now being made to rediscover the high period of Victorian Queenstown, when it was the last point of departure from Ireland for emigrant ships — and luxury liners — bound for the New World.

Thursday Déardaoin Donnerstag Jeudi

29

Friday Aoine Freitag Vendredi

30

Saturday Satharn Samstag Samedi

31

Sunday Domhnach Sonntag Dimanche

1

1993

AUGUST

Monday Luan Montag Lundi ● Week 32
Bank & public holiday

2

Tuesday Máirt Dienstag Mardi

3

Wednesday Céadaoin Mittwoch Mercredi

4

THE POINT DEPOT, NORTH WALL
Dublin

Thursday Déardaoin Donnerstag Jeudi

5

The Midland Great Western goods depot on the North Wall, dating from 1875, is one of the better buildings along the River Liffey. Neo-classical in style, it is the most recent of Dublin's fine collection of Victorian railway stations, though, like Broadstone and Harcourt Street, it became surplus to CIE's requirements. However, it found a new use as a major entertainment venue after a costly renovation by dockland entrepreneur Harry Crosbie, in collaboration with Apollo Leisure. It is a pity, however, that the building had to be turned around back-to-front, with a huge metal-clad flytower riding over its fine facade.

Friday Aoine Freitag Vendredi

6

Saturday Satharn Samstag Samedi

7

Sunday Domhnach Sonntag Dimanche

8

1993   AUGUST

Monday Luan Montag Lundi ● Week 33

9

Tuesday Máirt Dienstag Mardi

10

Wednesday Céadaoin Mittwoch Mercredi

11

Thursday Déardaoin Donnerstag Jeudi

12

Friday Aoine Freitag Vendredi

13

Saturday Satharn Samstag Samedi

14

Sunday Domhnach Sonntag Dimanche

15

SWEENEY'S HOTEL
Oughterard, Co. Galway

Oughterard is almost like an oasis in the otherwise bleak landscape of Connemara. In medieval times, it was controlled by the ferocious O'Flahertys, who so scourged the city of Galway that its west gate bore the inscription: "From the fury of the O'Flaherty's, Good Lord deliver us." Nowadays, Oughterard is better known as an angling centre, given its location near the shores of Lough Corrib. One of the favourite haunts of anglers is Sweeney's Hotel, a much-extended Georgian house pleasantly situated opposite a great stand of trees lining the Owenriff River which runs through the village.

Lúnasa • August • Août

1993

AUGUST

Monday Luan Montag Lundi • Week 34

16

Tuesday Máirt Dienstag Mardi

17

Wednesday Céadaoin Mittwoch Mercredi

18

BISHOP'S GATE
Downhill, Co. Derry

Frederick Augustus Hervey (1730-1803), the Earl Bishop of Derry, was an immensely wealthy art collector, builder and womaniser, who spent much of his time in Italy indulging in his various passions. At home, one of the more preposterous of his projects was a palace at Downhill, on the windswept north coast of Co. Derry, where he also built the famous Mussenden Temple as well as a mausoleum in memory of his late brother, whom he had succeeded as 4th Earl of Bristol in 1779. Though the house is just a shell following a disastrous fire in 1851, the temple and this lodge — known as Bishop's Gate — are in the care of the National Trust.

Thursday Déardaoin Donnerstag Jeudi

19

Friday Aoine Freitag Vendredi

20

Saturday Satharn Samstag Samedi

21

Sunday Domhnach Sonntag Dimanche

22

Monday Luan Montag Lundi ● Week 35

23

Tuesday Máirt Dienstag Mardi

24

Wednesday Céadaoin Mittwoch Mercredi

25

CONWAY'S BAR
Ramelton, Co. Donegal

Ramelton is one of the Plantation towns of East Donegal, founded by Sir William Stewart. Its location on the River Leannan, which feeds into Lough Swilly, was the key to its prosperity, as Alistair Rowan notes in his book on the architectural heritage of North-West Ulster. By the early nineteenth century it had its own corn mill, brewery, linen works and bleach greens, and some of this industry is exemplified by the fine row of warehouses along the river. Behind the harbour is this single-storey bar, typically rural in character, which enjoys all the attributes pub designers seek in their efforts to recreate the traditional Irish pub.

Thursday Déardaoin Donnerstag Jeudi

26

Friday Aoine Freitag Vendredi

27

Saturday Satharn Samstag Samedi

28

Sunday Domhnach Sonntag Dimanche

29

1993 AUGUST-SEPTEMBER

Monday Luan Montag Lundi ● Week 36

30

Tuesday Máirt Dienstag Mardi

31

Wednesday Céadaoin Mittwoch Mercredi

1

GREAT SOUTH WALL
Dublin Port

Thursday Déardaoin Donnerstag Jeudi

2

The construction of the Great South Wall was the largest single engineering feat of Dublin's Golden Age in the eighteenth century. It was sorely needed to provide shelter from south-easterly gales for shipping in the city's rapidly expanding port, and its impact on the tidal flows in the bay was so enormous that it contributed to the creation of the Bull Island, now a UN-designated "biosphere reserve", fringed by the ever-popular Dollymount Strand. Halfway along is the Half-Moon bathing place, facing the old fishing village of Ringsend and the Poolbeg power station. It's also a bracing route to walk at almost any time of the year.

Friday Aoine Freitag Vendredi

3

Saturday Satharn Samstag Samedi

4

Sunday Domhnach Sonntag Dimanche

5

1993 SEPTEMBER

Monday Luan Montag Lundi ● Week 37

6

Tuesday Máirt Dienstag Mardi

7

Wednesday Céadaoin Mittwoch Mercredi

8

Thursday Déardaoin Donnerstag Jeudi

9

Friday Aoine Freitag Vendredi

10

Saturday Satharn Samstag Samedi

11

Sunday Domhnach Sonntag Dimanche

12

CUSTOM HOUSE
Limerick

Seven years ago, when he took over as *de facto* Limerick city architect, the redoubtable Jim Barrett decided that he was going to have a mission: quite simply, to turn the city around to face the River Shannon. It seemed like an impossible dream; but, since then, the pieces have been falling into place — the pedestrian bridge over the Abbey River, the restored Potato Market, the Civic Offices, the public park at Arthur's Quay and the restoration of King John's Castle, with its gutsy visitor centre. Now another crucial element is being added, with the late eighteenth-century Custom House converted to house the hugely varied Hunt Collection.

1993 **SEPTEMBER**

Monday Luan Montag Lundi ● Week 38

13

Tuesday Máirt Dienstag Mardi

14

Wednesday Céadaoin Mittwoch Mercredi

15

TRAWLER AT ROUNDSTONE
Co. Galway

Roundstone is bluntly described as a ''decayed fishing village'' in *The Shell Guide to Ireland*. As Peter Harbison notes, it was developed in the 1820s by the exotically named harbour engineer Alexander Nimmo, and settled with fisher-folk from Scotland. It was also visited by that early tourist to Ireland, William Makepeace Thackeray, who came to see Victorian justice being dispensed in this remote part of the kingdom. Inland is Roundstone Bog, the last surviving wilderness area in Connemara, which was the focus of controversy a few years ago over plans by local business interests to build an airport on its perimeter, near Clifden.

Thursday Déardaoin Donnerstag Jeudi

16

Friday Aoine Freitag Vendredi

17

Saturday Satharn Samstag Samedi

18

Sunday Domhnach Sonntag Dimanche

19

1993   SEPTEMBER

Monday Luan Montag Lundi ● Week 39

20

Tuesday Máirt Dienstag Mardi

21

Wednesday Céadaoin Mittwoch Mercredi

22

Thursday Déardaoin Donnerstag Jeudi

23

Friday Aoine Freitag Vendredi

24

Saturday Satharn Samstag Samedi

25

Sunday Domhnach Sonntag Dimanche

26

**GLENDALOUGH
Co. Wicklow**

Saint Kevin certainly knew how to pick a tranquil place in which to build his monastery. The foundation he established dates from the sixth century and his cell, by the Upper Lake, can still be seen today. Located in the most beautiful valley of Co. Wicklow, Glendalough flourished, despite frequent plundering, until 1398, when it was destroyed by English forces. However, the site continued to be a place of pilgrimage and, in recent decades, of tourism. In 1989 the Office of Public Works opened an interpretative centre in Glendalough, though some visitors feel that the monastic remains — which include a round tower and small cathedral — are somewhat overshadowed by it.

1993 SEPTEMBER-OCTOBER

Monday Luan Montag Lundi ● Week 40

27

Tuesday Máirt Dienstag Mardi

28

Wednesday Céadaoin Mittwoch Mercredi

29

BUTCHER'S SHOP
Navan, Co. Meath

Every book on Irish
shopfronts in recent years
— and there have been
quite a few — makes the
point that the choice of
colour is not entirely
coincidental. Thus,
jewellers tended to choose
black, the vegetable shops
green (not surprisingly)
and the butchers red
(again, for obvious
reasons). This shop in
Navan doesn't quite
conform, being
''scumbled'' rather than
painted, but the red-and-
white stripes (the basis of
the barber's pole) are still
visible — and, in any case,
it's a pork-and-bacon
outlet, not beef and lamb.
One very comforting
feature is the evidence of
habitation over the shop in
the lace curtains on the
first-floor windows.

Thursday Déardaoin Donnerstag Jeudi

30

Friday Aoine Freitag Vendredi

1

Saturday Satharn Samstag Samedi

2

Sunday Domhnach Sonntag Dimanche

3

Monday Luan Montag Lundi ● Week 41

4

Tuesday Máirt Dienstag Mardi

5

Wednesday Céadaoin Mittwoch Mercredi

6

GOVERNMENT BUILDINGS
Dublin

Dubliners have a great knack for thinking up nicknames to puncture the pretensions of the powers-that-be. And there can be few edifices on which they have employed their skills to more memorable effect than Government Buildings, following its restoration in 1991 by the then Taoiseach, Charles J. Haughey — a personal "grand projet" which cost £17.5 million. Almost immediately, the rather pompous Edwardian complex was dubbed the Chas Mahal, otherwise Château Charlemagne, or, more wickedly, Teach Ceausescu. Then, as soon as Albert Reynolds took over as Taoiseach in February 1992, it was instantly renamed the Albert Hall.

Thursday Déardaoin Donnerstag Jeudi

7

Friday Aoine Freitag Vendredi

8

Saturday Satharn Samstag Samedi

9

Sunday Domhnach Sonntag Dimanche

10

1993   OCTOBER

Monday Luan Montag Lundi ● Week 42

11

Tuesday Máirt Dienstag Mardi

12

Wednesday Céadaoin Mittwoch Mercredi

13

KNOCKBREDA PARISH CHURCH
Belfast

Precious little has survived from Belfast's Georgian era. Much of it suffered from redevelopment during the Victorian period, when Belfast was at its zenith, and a lot of what survived fell victim to the redevelopment boom of the 1960s and later. Knockbreda Parish Church, being far removed from the hectic pace of ''progress'' in the city centre, still graces its elevated site and is sustained by a large congregation drawn from this relatively prosperous suburb. It dates from 1747 and was designed by Richard Cassels, the premier architect of the mid eighteenth century, whose credits include the Rotunda Hospital, Leinster House and Powerscourt.

Thursday Déardaoin Donnerstag Jeudi

14

Friday Aoine Freitag Vendredi

15

Saturday Satharn Samstag Samedi

16

Sunday Domhnach Sonntag Dimanche

17

1993   OCTOBER

Monday Luan Montag Lundi ● Week 43

18

Tuesday Máirt Dienstag Mardi

19

Wednesday Céadaoin Mittwoch Mercredi

20

COTTAGE
Mannin Bay, Co. Galway

Very few of the modern bungalows which now litter the rural landscape, North and South, have made much of an effort to fit into their surroundings. Perhaps this is not surprising, since so many of the bungalow-builders seem to want to make their mark on the countryside — even in their choice of showy suburban gardens. They might have paid more attention to the humbler dwellings of old and how they were almost married to the landscape, like this cottage at Mannin Bay, between Ballyconneely and Clifden, in Connemara. Set well back from the road within a random lacework of dry stone walls, it is almost an object lesson on how to do it.

Thursday Déardaoin Donnerstag Jeudi

21

Friday Aoine Freitag Vendredi

22

Saturday Satharn Samstag Samedi

23

Sunday Domhnach Sonntag Dimanche

24

1993   OCTOBER

Monday Luan Montag Lundi • Week 44
Bank & public holiday

25

Tuesday Máirt Dienstag Mardi

26

Wednesday Céadaoin Mittwoch Mercredi

27

ORNAMENTAL GATES, FOTA
Co. Cork

Instead of being celebrated as one of Cork's finest amenities, Fota has been the focus of a long-running battle in recent years over the fate of the house, its arboretum and the extensive estate. Formerly the seat of the Smith-Barrys, the neo-classical house was largely created by the Morrisons in the early nineteenth century; they also designed these ornamental garden gates. And though the house was restored in recent years by Cork businessman Richard Wood, in order to hang his collection of landscapes there, it had to be closed to the public later because UCC, which bought Fota from the last of the Smith-Barrys in 1975, had failed to maintain it.

Thursday Déardaoin Donnerstag Jeudi

28

Friday Aoine Freitag Vendredi

29

Saturday Satharn Samstag Samedi

30

Sunday Domhnach Sonntag Dimanche

31

Monday Luan Montag Lundi ● Week 45

1

Tuesday Máirt Dienstag Mardi

2

Wednesday Céadaoin Mittwoch Mercredi

3

Thursday Déardaoin Donnerstag Jeudi

4

Friday Aoine Freitag Vendredi

5

Saturday Satharn Samstag Samedi

6

Sunday Domhnach Sonntag Dimanche

7

McGONAGLES BARBER SHOP
Limavady, Co. Derry

After the sustained assault from ''unisex'' hairdressers and other trendy coiffure establishments, it is always surprising to find that any traditional barbers have survived. Here, in Irish Green Street, Limavady, is the Real McCoy, complete with red-and-white striped pole over the door. This feature harks back to the days when barbers doubled as surgeons and the only anaesthetic their patients had was to hang on tightly to the pole. But in McGonagles, as in other surviving men's barbers, the operations carried out nowadays are likely to be confined to ''short back and sides'', with a dash of Brylcreem to finish it off.

Monday Luan Montag Lundi ● Week 46

8

Tuesday Máirt Dienstag Mardi

9

Wednesday Céadaoin Mittwoch Mercredi

10

PORTUMNA CASTLE
Co. Galway

Semi-fortified houses, complete with castellations and gunports, were a feature of the various Plantations in Ireland during the late sixteenth and early seventeenth centuries — indicating a degree of insecurity on the part of their owners. Portumna Castle, one of the largest examples of this type of defensible architecture, was built circa 1615 by Richard Burke, 4th Earl of Clanrickarde, who was well connected with the English court and served as Governor of Connacht. The castle, approached through no less than three sets of gates, was gutted by an accidental fire in 1826 and remained a ruin until it was re-roofed recently by the Office of Public Works.

Thursday Déardaoin Donnerstag Jeudi

11

Friday Aoine Freitag Vendredi

12

Saturday Satharn Samstag Samedi

13

Sunday Domhnach Sonntag Dimanche

14

1993 NOVEMBER

Monday Luan Montag Lundi ● Week 47

15

Tuesday Máirt Dienstag Mardi

16

Wednesday Céadaoin Mittwoch Mercredi

17

FORMER PRESBYTERIAN MEETING HOUSE
Eustace Street, Dublin

Believed to date from around 1720, this stucco-fronted former meeting house — not at all typical of austere Presbyterian architecture — is one of the oldest surviving buildings in the Temple Bar area of Dublin. Less than fifteen years ago it was actually threatened with demolition to extend a large surface carpark into Eustace Street, but its listed status averted this unseemly fate. For many years, the meeting house served as Brindley's printing works and, though in an appalling state after years of neglect, it is now being restored to provide a children's theatre in the heart of Temple Bar's cultural quarter. How times change.

Thursday Déardaoin Donnerstag Jeudi

18

Friday Aoine Freitag Vendredi

19

Saturday Satharn Samstag Samedi

20

Sunday Domhnach Sonntag Dimanche

21

1993   NOVEMBER

Monday Luan Montag Lundi ● Week 48

22

Tuesday Máirt Dienstag Mardi

23

Wednesday Céadaoin Mittwoch Mercredi

24

WHELAN'S SHOP
Main Street, Wexford

Those evocative Lawrence Collection photographs of Irish towns in the late nineteenth century usually show a continuous run of Victorian shopfronts, many with canvas awnings. Wexford's narrow North Main Street and South Main Street, mercifully spared road-widening in recent decades, had quite a few fine shopfronts until the 1960s, when, as in other Irish towns, far too many were sacrificed for plastic tat. All over the country, publicans and shopkeepers have been scrambling to restore the *status quo ante* with decidedly mixed results, and Wexford now has more than its fair share of mock-Victorian ''replicas''.

Thursday Déardaoin Donnerstag Jeudi

25

Friday Aoine Freitag Vendredi

26

Saturday Satharn Samstag Samedi

27

Sunday Domhnach Sonntag Dimanche

28

1993 NOVEMBER-DECEMBER

Monday Luan Montag Lundi ● Week 49

29

Tuesday Máirt Dienstag Mardi

30

Wednesday Céadaoin Mittwoch Mercredi

1

GAZEBO, MALLOW CASTLE
Co. Cork

Follies are a whimsical feature of many a country estate, in Ireland no less than in Britain. They suggest a life of blissful indolence on the part of the landed aristocracy, though, in some cases, the grander and more fanciful follies were commissioned as famine-relief projects by comparatively caring landlords. Ireland's most spectacular example is the Connolly Folly, equidistant from Castletown and Carton, in Co. Kildare. By comparison, this octagonal gazebo in the grounds of Mallow Castle, Co. Cork, is very domestic in scale, barely big enough to serve as a potting shed or, perhaps, a drinks dispenser on hot summer days.

Thursday Déardaoin Donnerstag Jeudi

2

Friday Aoine Freitag Vendredi

3

Saturday Satharn Samstag Samedi

4

Sunday Domhnach Sonntag Dimanche

5

1993 **DECEMBER**

Monday Luan Montag Lundi ● Week 50

6

Tuesday Máirt Dienstag Mardi

7

Wednesday Céadaoin Mittwoch Mercredi

8

Thursday Déardaoin Donnerstag Jeudi

9

Friday Aoine Freitag Vendredi

10

Saturday Satharn Samstag Samedi

11

Sunday Domhnach Sonntag Dimanche

12

SOUTHWELL CHARITY
Downpatrick, Co. Down

Downpatrick is still off the beaten track, even though it reputedly contains the last resting place of Ireland's patron saint, which ought to have made it more important. But this has enabled the quiet town in Co. Down to escape the worst excesses of the modern age and to hold onto its heritage. The town's many fine eighteenth-century buildings include the Southwell Charity, an almshouse and school for the poor founded in 1733 by Edward Southwell, which is still in use more than two-and-a-half centuries later. Surmounted by a distinctive quadrangular cupola, the building is regarded as a good example of Irish Palladian architecture.

1993 DECEMBER

Mí na Nollag • Dezember • Décembre

Monday Luan Montag Lundi • Week 51 — **13**

Tuesday Máirt Dienstag Mardi — **14**

Wednesday Céadaoin Mittwoch Mercredi — **15**

Thursday Déardaoin Donnerstag Jeudi — **16**

Friday Aoine Freitag Vendredi — **17**

Saturday Satharn Samstag Samedi — **18**

Sunday Domhnach Sonntag Dimanche — **19**

SAWMILL
Slane, Co. Meath

Slane will always be associated with its castle, seat of the Earl of Mount Charles, and the hugely successful rock concerts he has promoted in its grounds by the banks of the Boyne — as well as the enormous fire which severely damaged the building in November 1991. But Slane, the estate village, has many other fine features — notably the four nearly identical Georgian houses which grace its crossroads and the impressive complex of eighteenth-century cut-stone mill buildings just below the Boyne bridge. Once the largest of its kind in Ireland, the Slane Mill is a fine relic of industrial archaeology, eminently suitable for restoration.

1993   **DECEMBER**

Monday Luan Montag Lundi ● Week 52

20

Tuesday Máirt Dienstag Mardi

21

Wednesday Céadaoin Mittwoch Mercredi

22

PUB
Clonaslee, Co. Laois

The Slieve Bloom
Mountains have been
designated as Ireland's
first "Environment Park",
which presumably means
an end to the policy of
covering the area with
conifers and then clear-
felling whole swathes of
forest when the trees
reach maturity. The park
should also help to put the
largely ignored Midlands
back on the map, at least
in tourism terms, and this
should benefit the little-
known villages in the
vicinity, which have
names like Drimmo,
Kinnity and Rosenallis. In
Clonaslee, on the Birr-
Mountmellick Road which
skirts the northern edge of
the mountain range, you
can slake your thirst in
M. D. Hickey's pretty
barge-boarded Bridge
House bar.

Thursday Déardaoin Donnerstag Jeudi

23

Friday Aoine Freitag Vendredi
Christmas Eve

24

Saturday Satharn Samstag Samedi
Christmas Day Lá Nollag

25

Sunday Domhnach Sonntag Dimanche
St Stephen's Day

26

Monday Luan Montag Lundi ● Week 53
Bank holiday

27

Tuesday Máirt Dienstag Mardi
Bank holiday

28

Wednesday Céadaoin Mittwoch Mercredi

29

JAMES JOYCE'S BIRTHPLACE
41 Brighton Square, Dublin

Notoriously, Dublin's most illustrious writer lived in numerous houses all over the city, declining in status over the years as his father's fortunes fell. Brighton Square illustrates how comfortable the family must have been when they started out, though it is, of course, a triangle rather than a square — just as geometrically incorrect as most of the Diamonds in Northern towns. A plaque on No. 41, typical of the red-brick Victorian houses built for Dublin's middle class, records the fact that Joyce was born there on 2 February 1882. Unlike Shaw's birthplace in Synge Street, it has been well maintained — as a private house, not a museum.

Thursday Déardaoin Donnerstag Jeudi

30

Friday Aoine Freitag Vendredi

31

Saturday Satharn Samstag Samedi
New Year's Day Lá Coille

1

Sunday Domhnach Sonntag Dimanche

2

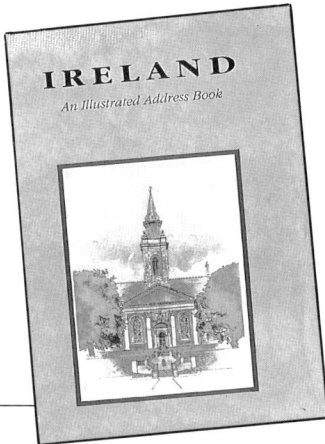

Ireland: An Illustrated Address Book
Illustrations by Kieran Doyle O'Brien

Colour plates illustrate aspects of Ireland's rich architectural heritage.

212 × 154mm/112pp/15 colour plates/ Hardback/ISBN 0 86281 294 1/IR£10.99

Get It Fixed In Ireland
Marion Fitzgerald

An essential reference book for every Irish household. A wide-ranging directory of services, shops and stores ready to come to your aid when things go wrong. Everything from where to get shirts mended, to fixing a leaky shower.

215 × 135mm/208pp/26 illustrations/ Paperback/ISBN 0 86281 303 4/IR£6.99

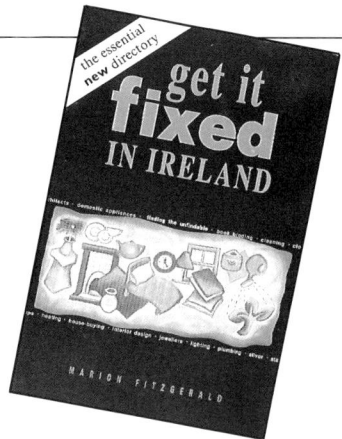

Ireland's Inland Waterways
Ruth Delany

An absorbing and fully illustrated story of Ireland's inland waterways, tracing their development from the 1730s right up to the present day.

'Its copious illustrations are marvellous.'   *Irish Times*

270 × 82mm/128pp/90 b&w illus/ ISBN 0 86281 200 3/IR£7.95

APPLETREE PRESS

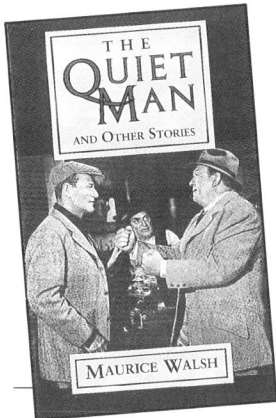

The Quiet Man and Other Stories
Maurice Walsh

Published originally as *Green Rushes* and long unavailable, the new edition of this classic collection, with its themes of nationalism, human dignity, honour and love, will be widely welcomed.

215 × 135mm/204pp/Paperback/ ISBN 0 86281 307 1/IR£6.99

Irish Battles:
A Military History of Ireland
G. A. Hayes-McCoy

This paperback edition presents a military history of Ireland in the form of a series of connected studies of major Irish battles, from 1014 to 1798. The standard work on Ireland's military history.

216 × 155mm/360pp/20 col. illus/ ISBN 0 86281 250 X/IR£8.95

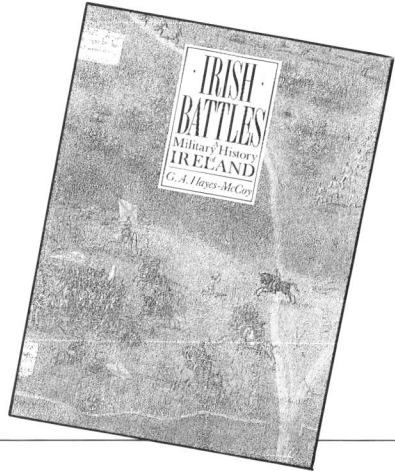

Standing Stones and
Other Monuments of Early Ireland
Kenneth McNally

Reissue, by popular demand, of this impressive study of Ireland's field monuments, with over 70 striking photographs of megalithic tombs, ritual circles and alignments; cult stones, raths and cashels; and crosses and round towers of the Celtic church.

260 × 184mm/128pp/b&w illus/ ISBN 0 86281 2011/IR£6.99

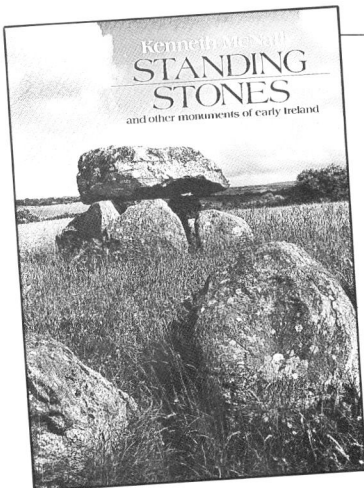